D1357997

I Feel Fall Weather

by Mari Schuh

first step nonfiction

Lerner Publications ◆ Minneapolis

Copyright © 2017 by Lerner Publishing Group, Inc.

The images in this book are used with the permission of: © iStockphoto.com/Lisa Thornberg, p. 4; © gillmar/Shutterstock.com, p. 5; © Subbotina Anna/Shutterstock.com, p. 6; © Sergieiev/Shutterstock.com, p. 7; © JGI/Jamie Grill/Getty Images, p. 8; ©iStockphoto.com/plushka, p. 9; © Ian Taylor/Design Pics/Getty Images, p. 10; ©Jaromir Chalabala/Shutterstock.com, p. 11; © iStockphoto.com/fishwork, p. 12; © MNStudio/Shutterstock.com, p. 13; © George W. Bailey/Shutterstock.com, p. 14; © Image Source/Getty Images, p. 15; © iStockphoto.com/rivendels, p. 16; ©Olesia Bilkei/Shutterstock.com, p. 17; © iStockphoto.com/emholk, p. 18; © iStockphoto.com/Christopher Badzioch, p. 19; © Kotenko Oleksandr/Shutterstock.com, p. 20; © Anne Ackermann/Getty Images, p. 21; © Echo/Getty Images, p. 22.
Front cover: © Image Source/SuperStock.

Main body text set in ITC Avant Garde Gothic Std Medium 21/25.
Typeface provided by International Typeface Corp.

Lerner Publications Company
A division of Lerner Publishing Group, Inc.
241 First Avenue North
Minneapolis, MN 55401 USA

For reading levels and more information, look up this title at www.lernerbooks.com.

Library of Congress Cataloging-in-Publication Data

Names: Schuh, Mari C., 1975– author.
Title: I feel fall weather / Mari Schuh.
Description: Minneapolis : Lerner Publications, [2016] | Series: First step nonfiction. Observing fall | Audience: Ages 5–8. | Audience: K to grade 3. | Includes index.
Identifiers: LCCN 2015036528| ISBN 9781512407976 (lb : alk. paper) | ISBN 9781512412123 (pb : alk. paper) | ISBN 9781512409932 (eb pdf)
Subjects: LCSH: Autumn—Juvenile literature. | Weather—Juvenile literature. | Seasons—Juvenile literature.
Classification: LCC QB637.7 .S38 2016 | DDC 508.2—dc23
LC record available at http://lccn.loc.gov/2015036528

Manufactured in the United States of America
1 – CG – 7/15/16

Table of Contents

Changes in Fall

Summer has ended.

Fall is here.

The sun sets earlier.

Days are shorter in the fall.

It gets dark earlier in the evening.

Weather changes in the fall.

Fall is cooler than summer.

The **temperature** drops. The air is cooler.

It feels **brisk**.

People can sometimes see their breath.

They wear jackets to stay warm.

Wind

Fall can be windy.

The wind blows fall leaves.

The wind feels cold. It is
strong.

Fall can be rainy.

Umbrellas help keep people dry.

People use umbrellas.

People jump in puddles.

They get wet!

Weather Differences

Fall can be cloudy.

Fall can be sunny too.

What do you like most about fall?

What is fall weather like where you live?

Glossary

brisk – fresh and cool

fall – the season after summer and before winter

temperature – how hot or cold something is

weather – the condition of the outside air at a certain place and time

Index